immortal rose

nicole rose

a huge thank you to every single soul who has allowed me to feel love
or pain
i thank you for the gift of feeling and the growth you have brought me
i owe my evolution to you

Nicole Rose

immortal rose

© 2020, Nicole Rose

Self-published

nicolesrosesl@gmail.com

contents

love

you know that feeling of fresh love. there is nothing like it. when you open its package and joy runs through your veins and it doesn't matter how much sleep you got the night before because their energy fuels you enough to run marathons. how your feet don't notice the potholes in the road because their voice is so smooth it fills in any bumps around you. even when you're out of breath it doesn't matter because you know at the end of the day that you get to be in sync with their lungs and it brings you happiness that no amount of flowers can buy. instead of flowers, you start to bloom instead, and strangers approach you about the glow that paints your face. this feeling is undeniably beautiful, and it makes you feel like everything around you is too. when it crashes and the newness of love begins to fade, i hope you realize the flowers of new life that await you have the potential to be just as beautiful. love may change, but it will never die.

we survived a death
of a love story
that wasn't finished
our souls were reborn
destined to meet again

when my senses
start to fall asleep
there is an alarm that lies in your touch

no one makes me feel alive like you

it's an honour
to listen to your heartbeat
to discover what makes it beat faster
and what makes it full
and my heart never gets tired of learning

she craved a love that was blind to the clock
and not each other
timeless and transparent

when i see the future
i grab my paintbrush
and place a blank canvas in front of me
i start with dipping my brush in black
and paint the night sky
then i grab yellow and paint the stars
then with the same colour
i start to connect them
and i see the constellations of you

love does not hide
it does not reveal itself
solely under perfect circumstances
it pours light
where darkness sleeps
it does not shatter
where things are broken
it fights for peace
when guns of vengeance try to overpower its force
it is romantic
and it is not
it is the one thing that mends the unbreakable
it makes life worth a shot

deep beneath the ocean
there is a depth that cannot compare
to how your soul touches me

when i hear your voice
i am deaf to the life around me
you are my favourite song

in the cold hard world
you remind me that i am still soft and warm-blooded
your aura melts the walls i've built around me

there is nothing sexier
than the burning tension
of what you discover after you've stripped each other's souls first
everything begins to feel more naked

after seeing the sight of you
day after day
i could go blind
and still be grateful
because to me
i'd seen the best there is to see

fast asleep
i felt your touch
in my dreams
when i opened my eyes
i felt my sixth sense come alive
do you feel me

dreaming of you

your soul is the glove
that keeps me warm
when the storms of life make me shiver
there is so much comfort in the temperature of you

tangle me in the sheets of your loyalty where trust will sew us in

you are the dream that never sleeps
my heart has stayed awake ever since it met the rhythm of your soul

your cologne lingers
in strands of my hair
my pillow falls asleep
to the scent of our love

when i look into your eyes
i see nostalgia
now
and the future
in every shade

there are connections so strong
that they lift the soul
and never lose their impact
no matter how long life goes on

there is lightning in my bones
that strikes when you caress me
you are the rain
in the desert
that quenches the winds of my heart

with tender lips
and a graceful heart
her love is one that imitates art
with every word she spoke
his senses awoke
his soft glance at her
as her eyes lit aglow
a peace they would never dare let go

your presence has impacted me so deeply
i'm convinced
if i never met you
i would permanently feel something missing

when i was still learning to love my constellations
you saw the galaxies in me
and made me believe
that maybe the universe needed my stars too

there is passion in our words
that longs to be released by our tongues

isn't it crazy
we spend a lifetime
trying to figure out life
but just a few seconds with you
and it all makes sense

it didn't feel like i fell for you
because to fall
is to let go of yourself
intentionally
i just walked my path
unapologetically myself
and you caught up with me
to hold my hand
and said
"let's roam these streets together and see where it takes us"
and not once
did i want to look back

there is a force of curiosity
that lives in the unknown
sliced with the knife of losing one's pride
it is only then
that love wins

the rays in your eyes
are brighter than those of the sun
when the rain comes undone
and the clouds separate from one
you are the rainbow i've been waiting for
after the skies of patience stop their pour

there exists a quiet feeling
that wraps around him
the noise of her gentle embrace
brushing against his skin
sends goosebumps down his spine

a love that speaks in silence

any conflicts we face
that i carry in my hands
i hold yours
and they dissolve

there are galaxies that live inside your eyes
that fill in the space
when life feels empty

as my breath fogged the glass
my first instinct
was to trace us

in the blur of life
i always see you

he lit a match
that the fire within her heart
would never forget

she wore her heart upon her sleeve
and he stripped away the fabric
to bare the beauty of her naked soul

no matter where life takes us
and who it brings us to
i cherish the fact that it gave me the chance to meet you
we are my favourite coincidence

let your lips rehearse
what your body will sing to me
as we make our music in harmony

he watched himself
slowly soften at the core of her being
as she peeled her layers
he embraced the skins that fell from her
like his own
he flashed back to when it all began with the seeds of her fruit
how he held them in his young hands
as she held a pot of water full of dreams
that soaked into the grounds they slowly built
each day the garden bloomed fonder
never running out of the harvest of their promises
an embodiment of some love stories
that plant their seed
are watered with patience
and get lucky enough to grow to the end

upon the sky
in the clouds
where raindrops form
and the bird sings its song below
its hymn travels to the ground
where flowers grow
and butterflies roam
while trees breathe their air
and the mountains still leave some beauty to spare

the creation of you

our love is nostalgic
two old souls feeding each other
oh lover from a past life
here we are again

when you find a love that's once in a lifetime
you fight so you don't have to look for it a second

as my mouth
came to the surface
gasping for air
your kiss calmed every inch of my lungs

you are the wave that washes the sands of my fears to shore
and every day i collect shells of security knowing you're by my side

i don't need to check the weather
because when i have you by my side
i know it's going to be a beautiful day

i want to bathe in your presence
and wash away our insecurities together

your voice sets my soul ablaze
and your kiss burns my fears away
it whispers like the rain that soothes me to sleep
and laughs like the song of winds
there is nothing that leaves your lips
that i do not love

you are the kind of love
that has me jotting down vows
as time passes by
longing for the days to live them
dressed in white

nicole rose

my petals only open
when they know you are watering me

our heartbeats overpower
the uproar of life's battles
we have made symphonies out of the chaos
and a chorus of joy repeats itself

you are a tree
as you change
i accept each fallen leaf
and i'm equally impressed
you are the season i never tire of

the butterflies i felt in my stomach
when we met
never learned how to fly away

"love will never have my back"
don't try to tell me it's mould will never crack or
that its shell will always stay intact
if you open up and dig beneath its surface you will find
there are tears and pride and values that collide
even if there are days that are filled with no hope
it winds up leaving your desires hanging on a rope
it's not true that
love offers hope
because
it brings happiness that is conditional
and damages our subliminal
it will never last forever
that's its nature
unpredictable like the weather
it is past my control
and you'll never hear me say
i believe in love

now read it backwards

pain

you tell me the timing is just not right
but time passes by
and there wasn't a day that passed where i wasn't ready to be with you
i tried to figure out what was so special about tomorrow
because love is always ready for today

you weren't

the one that i'm wasting this ink on
probably stopped thinking of me long ago
but if i can touch you with this pen
i hope to stain your heart instead

"i love you"
"i love you more"
"let's agree to disagree"
you left me
i whisper
"i love you more"
i was left with my own echo

i won the battle i was afraid of

the what ifs are constantly treading in waters of what is
i try to tell them to swim back to shore
but they refuse
just in case you'd come save them

your mind is talking about me
while your mouth speaks to her
my mind is talking about you
while my mouth speaks to him

why did we let our lips win

to stop loving you
was like putting ice into boiling water
and asking it not to melt

impossible

i miss the way my brain soaked in your good mornings like a sponge
i've had to squeeze out every ounce of love you once gave me
convincing myself you were never the one
today feels dry
as i soak in this goodbye

i once dreamed of being a girl who couldn't feel
who felt cursed
while i observed the blessings of the dull
as they went about their day
while i struggled to filter what my brain had to say
how my mind stayed as busy
as the revolving earth
constantly turning
with no gravity to hold it down
as i watched the planets float around me
they seemed to be still
stiller than i
so out of reach
i could never touch them
let alone be them
but maybe i was meant to feel the tide of all my stars
to truly make sense out of the constellations
maybe that is my calling

i used to be afraid of the dark
until i lost you
and now i fear the light
because then it is clear
you are no longer beside me

do not call me home
and treat me like a hotel
do not rest your eyes
on bed sheets
you do not plan to keep

the strings of my heart
bind onto you
and no matter how far i walk away
no one has cut the way i feel

sure, there're other hands to hold
but they touch my fingertips and not my soul

the hole i dug with distractions
after you left the grounds of me
forced me to garden in new ways
i tried the soil of him
i tried the soil of hating you
i tried the soil of keeping busy
but all i'm left with is the water
from the plants of my eyes

lost in the petals of
he loves me he loves me not
she craved a love she didn't have to question

the love you used to love me with
lies in a casket
but i still visit every day
in hopes i can bring it back to life
because the love i loved you with
is still alive well and breathing

you sewed me a veil
that sweeps the floor
where your feet no longer know
you've married my mind
and left the rest of me at the altar

when we ended
your heart was so open to let her in
but mine stayed closed
rejecting the keys that attempted their chances
locked to the hope of your return

tried to get high off the past
but my new life blew out the smoke
now i'm just left with transparent eyes
and a tired heart that's broke

i cried tears
that made a river
i would have swam to you
but my pride let me drown

my eyes close
hoping that one day they'll open to a world they're proud of
with you in it
and me with clear vision
that's a lot to ask of my eyelids
but underneath lies a bed to the eyes of a dreamer
that begs for its romanticized reality to be seen

immortal rose

we are two roses
growing
in opposite gardens
maybe one day
you'll plant a seed in mine

we never truly lost each other
we just lost time together
but it's all made up for in my mind

even though we no longer touch
i hope my words cling to you

the truth stands between us
as we stand around
too prideful to pick it up
circling it with what ifs
vulnerability screaming in my ear
"you can pick it up"
my mouth shakes
fear of regret pounds in my heart
i cannot leave it there
unsettled
will it make me weak
am i less for wanting to know

no

because i'd rather be lifted by the truth
than be burdened by a lie

you toy with my emotions
and you play the victim
as your arrogance rolls the dice
handing me cards of false hope
i spin the wheel
my mind spirals in whys
why

am i just a game to you

nicole rose

i miss fresh love
with no baggage
just empty bags
filled with pure intention

we fell in love
just to fall apart
but i guess that's the beauty of trying
to have the courage to stand at the top of a building
and jump together knowing
they could let go at any moment

busy days almost fool my mind
into thinking you do not have a place in it anymore
the days on the calendar that are empty
remind me how much space you still fill

when i hear your name
i used to hear bells
but now it rings
the music of us
that could have been

i'm so confident in what we had
that i could go years without speaking to you
but the moment the silence breaks

i know we'd feel like yesterday all over again

i'm bleeding for what my veins don't understand
how can you love the one who cut you
and reject those who offer band-aids

maybe the stars did align for us
but we are blind to the fact that we were meant to shine separately

it's been too long to feel the way i feel
too many days of telling myself maybe tomorrow i'll feel differently
but today is today again and i'm still ready to love you like it was the
beginning all over again

my body needs breaks
my mind needs breaks
but when it's time to tell my heart to take a break
it cannot rest knowing you exist

i'm tired of loveless flings
that fill voids but don't end in rings

she craved a ride or die type of love
but she always seemed to die of a broken heart instead

i stopped telling my heart to move on
it just doesn't understand
i'll die loving you
my mind will learn to live with it

dear her
i hope you know you hold everything i want
that you kiss the lips that spoke words to me that made me fall
that you wake up next to the real-life version of my dreams
that you keep my other half next to your pillow
as i freeze
as i wait
in hopes he'll remember how warm i made him
you are so lucky to get to love the love i wasn't finished loving
but he has chosen you
so take good care of him
as i try to accept that you are his blanket instead

even at my lowest points
i still get some highs
from the thought of you

i'm tired of chasing
because love never runs
it isn't supposed to leave you out of breath
or run down
it walks
alongside you
and holds your hand
and it only lets go when you need space
not when it feels like you don't deserve it
i hope we find a love that walks

why does heartbreak hurt?

it's all the good news you've been hiding inside for months
not wanting to waste your breath and tell them because they've
already moved on
it's the future and the events you planned together that are
permanently cancelled
and there is no rescheduling
it's telling your heart that yes they once loved you but they woke up
one morning and decided not to anymore
it's looking at those who have what you wanted with them
and thinking "we were so close to that"
it's music and listening differently because now you've lived enough
to relate to lyrics you used to hear happily
it's wanting to forget so bad that the act of trying to forget makes you
remember more
it's tears that fight with pride
that fight with knowing you deserve better
it's falling asleep to the dream of them and waking up to the reality

this is why the heart won't heal

every time i grab my brush
and paint my idea of you
reality grabs my hand
and says
"leave this to me"
"i'll finish"

i was blind to what i didn't want to see
because my vision was sharp on the days you loved me right

our love
used to come alive on sheets of white
but now that it has died
i'm left with these sheets of white
where my hand thinks of you

your lips were stained with beautiful promises
you couldn't help but try on a new shade
so you kissed her as they turned into lies
and you transfer the colours back onto me
and utter the words "i love you"
i would open my mouth to say it back
but i refuse to be a product of your uncertainty

i filled your heart with my blood
a donor of affection
until the void you had
was filled
and you used my fuel to drive away
and pump the love i craved from you into someone else

i don't want a love that makes me practice how strong i am when it
leaves
i want a love that makes me practice how good i am at loving while it
stays

the flashbacks
send chills
running down my back
my body craves the moments
my mind doesn't want back

i miss how we loved
with our lips wide open
you used to use them to kiss me
then they hurt me
with the words that fell from them
then you left
and now they're sealed

you ripped apart my dreams of us
and use them as a blanket
where you and her lie
as i lie on the floor
traced with our old footsteps
and try to be okay with that

what does silence hear?
it hears muffled cries in clean sheets
turned damp by my sorrow
it hears the voices in my head
that replay memories like its favourite film
it hears the faint voice of you
that fades more each day as i try to forget your sound
and what do we hear?

the silence of our pride

star-crossed lovers
but i still cross my fingers when i see the stars
that one day that may change

when they ask me
is your heart still broken?
i say
ask him
he's still holding a piece

i waited for you in sunsets
in the rises and falls of each passing day
in the sun that gave me hope
in the stars that i wished on every night
in the clouds that accept that storms never last
and getting lost in space
that one day we could

i wonder if i ever cross your mind
because every time my brain goes through its memories
its first stop is always you

you can pick up the gifts you gave me
and drive far away
but you can never pick up the part of you
you left in me

i knew it was you
when i'd sleep next to him
and you'd show up uninvited in my dreams
i knew it was you
when he kissed me
and i didn't want to open my eyes
because somehow the memory of you always overpowered what was
right in front of me
i knew it was you
when he talked of the future
and i panicked
because deep down i wanted it to be us in the end
i knew it was you
when he left me
and my heart still broke over you

my hands are tired from all the poems i wrote
but the hands i write about
aren't coming back
to soothe them

self-love

i hope you find a self-love
that shows up at your door when they don't
i hope it's the first validation you go to
when the world lets you feel small
i hope you don't let it shatter like a vase
in the tired hands of those who cannot appreciate what they hold
i hope it cradles you when the nights are long
and the love you crave from others falls short
i hope you know that you have it in you
you will be with yourself alive or dead
i hope you realize your own love is so powerful
it can turn immortal if you let it

to all the beautiful hearts that go unnoticed
because of eyes that have been dyed in warped ideals of beauty

you are not less

trying to make me jealous
is the equivalent of showing a bird you can run
i know who i am
my wings are not threatened by your legs

stop giving them so much power over you. it's one thing to be sad and human but it's another to let them take your worth with them and to let your thoughts of them consume you. that's like saying you hurt me so now i'm gonna hurt myself, and the people in my life and every action i take is because of you. you're gonna break down while you watch them have a breakthrough? you're going to let them have their win-win? i don't think so. love can blind you, but please be smart enough to see the truth. you are the truth, you are the best thing that will ever happen to you, you are worthy, and you must love yourself regardless if they do or not. you do not need to fight, or beg, or burn yourself out so they know your greatness. if they can't see the beautiful person you are, they weren't meant to. let them find their people while you find yours.

immortal rose

there is not a single person
who can tell me
who i am
if you don't walk in my shoes
you don't get to speak for my mouth

i wish you could meet the girl who grew because you left
but you don't deserve her

plant love inside yourself
without looking at how fast the flowers around you are sprouting
bloom at your own pace

that is enough

being beautiful is losing its value
be rememberable
sparkling eyes do not prevail over a dull mind

the world feeds on the insecure
spoon by spoon
it tells you why you can't be this
and why you should be more like that
and you digest it
and slowly it is all your stomach knows
but maybe the diet you need
isn't the one that's proclaimed by the seemingly perfect
maybe it's to stop eating up what they tell you to be
maybe it's time you start controlling what is fed to you
to feed yourself with what nourishes your soul
with your kindness with your self-talk
with all the self-love that has waited to be tasted
it is only then that you will experience truly feeling full

when you left
my value didn't walk with you
all the kind things you used to tell me
they're still true

i am deserving of my own happily ever after
i do not have to live vicariously through movies and fairytales
there is a crown of happiness waiting on the stairs of going after what i
want

the race of realizing your worth
cannot begin if you keep letting red flags slide

we cannot begin to change our world
and paint beautiful colours
with an angry palette
start by accepting your colours
and you'll see how you camouflage everyone in your path

i am not made for pleasure
or a body for lonely hands
to dispose of baggage you couldn't sort
or a quick meal for your eyes
or when your stomach desires
a late-night craving that's convenient
i am more than what meets the organ
i am the flesh
and everything behind it
more importantly

i am everything that is behind it

the mirror is not a reflection of all that you are
so stop giving it power
the stretch marks
the rolls
the scars
that mark your body
can't tell you about all the times you've made someone's day
when your love made a positive impact on lives
when your advice soothed the struggling

you are so much more than what a piece of glass tells you

i may not know everything
but i know my worth
and that's half the battle

to sail the seas of healing
you must stop swimming in the hate that sinks the boat of potential

when they laugh at your dreams
tell them not to worry
they do not have to carry your willpower on their back

if my worries could talk they would say
"i care about us"
"i care about what we do so much because i care about everything being ok in the end. that's all i want for you, and i'm sorry if it keeps you up at night, i'm sorry if it's made you cancel plans, i'm sorry if it's made you see yourself negatively, i'm sorry if it's made you think that others don't like you. i'm working on it because i hope we win in the end and that every second you spend doubting yourself because of me works out in your favour. it's only because i want you to get the interview, your dream career, the love of your life. i want all your goals to happen for you. i really do. i'm sorry for all the hurt i've caused along the way, but deep down i've always rooted for you or i never would have bothered to ignite this overwhelming fire in you."

she wore crowns of innocence
as he picked away at her jewels
she thought she lost her sparkle
and yearned for the taste of renewal
but she glistened all along
her value could never be wrong

i am not my body
i am everything my body allows me to do
it stands proud for me
it stands up for me
it fights for what it loves
while it defends against illness
it bleeds when it is broken
but its hands put on the band-aids to heal
it rests
and wakes up and finds the strength every day and says i can make this
work
it is its own healer

protector

miracle

tell me
what's to hate about that?

i strive to love myself in all the ways you didn't

stop waiting for them to come to their senses

come to your own
see the good in everything
feel how the change is changing you
hear the peace in the silence
taste the freedom that liberates you
hold the hands of those who deserve your company

i refuse to water myself down
because my truth is too strong for you to drink

your validation
does nothing
but confirm what i already admire about me
it is appreciated
but never needed

another chance
why?
so you can show your true colours on a repeated canvas?
i'll paint my story without you
no thanks

nicole rose

i'm not going to quiet my opinion
so your ego can be loud

the people in your life should see your worth

not be it

don't let them tell you your self-love is something to be ashamed of
ask them "have you ever loved someone?"
they will reply "yes"
tell them "what's wrong with doing the same for myself?"

i will not lower my voice to protect your ego
i will not dim my sugar to protect your salt
if you choose to stay bitter
it's not my tongue's fault

keep climbing
mountains are intimidated by the heights of your perseverance

know when to distinguish between pride and self-respect
it's not the fear of rejection
it's knowing
you deserve better than to chase what doesn't want to be caught

learn to develop a no matter what mentality
no matter what happens
no matter what they say
no matter if they judge
no matter if they stop seeing my worth
no matter if they leave

i will always matter to me
and they
do not have a say in that

we all want to be spoon-fed love
but as soon as it comes time to feed ourselves
starving becomes easier
without hesitation
let us grip the spoons
that will quiet our own stomachs

don't waste your breath
on those who pollute your mind
be kind to your environment

sometimes i just need to put a record on
show a little more skin
and remind myself to cherish the home i'm in
my own company is sexy

imagine if we focused more on the wonders of the world
rather than focusing on what's wrong with it
imagine

how beautiful the effects would be if you applied the same mentality
to yourself

i don't need you to pump validation in me
the ability to thrive runs through my veins
with or without you

look at the earth
how it breathes through the wind
and cries through the sky
how it shakes when it's uneasy
everything about the planet is human
allow yourself to be too

catch me dead waiting for you to act right
i'll just find someone who doesn't need to act

before you chase
make sure you've run the same distance for yourself

she dances on cold pavement
naked in the night
no hardship fazes her
she endures the good fight
no winds can shake her
no storms can break her
she's invincible to the seasons of life
she doesn't crumble due to strife
and on the top of her head
lies the crown of independence
she knows no fear
she's made friends with vengeance

i used to watch you in love with me
and be jealous
why can't i love myself like that?
now you're gone
and i'm following your footsteps
and now you're jealous
of how i love me the way you used to

the most extraordinary plot twist

if you're not trying to be found by me
stay lost
i am a treasure
i don't need to feel like i'm hunting for you

nicole rose

i need food water and air
notice how you're missing from the list?
humble yourself

if i can't give it to myself
i consider it a want
not a need

perfect is a word that only exists on paper
don't waste your time trying to make it come to life

leave it in the dictionary

i am a burning match
in a world full of candles
when the world blows on my fire
and i feel like burning out

i look at all the candles i've ignited
and i am glowing again

she's been a victim and a villain
and a human all the same
do not judge how she flies
she's learnt her worth but never in vain

stop making excuses for people
who make it clear they want to be excused
from the table of your life

there are so many versions of you running around
don't try to keep up with every perception
their opinion of you is their business only

everything that breaks has the ability to be pieced back together
the glue is in your will to believe it first

the spaces in your pores

the spaces in between your scars

the spaces in between your hips where you examine the structure of
your bones

the spaces in between sentences when your voice shakes and you want
to speak your mind

feed those spaces with love
let love in this time

if you cannot love me for everything that i am
no problem

i'll gladly take your place

nicole rose

i am a soul attached to a body
with lungs that breathe for adventure
whether you want to hold my hand or not
i will be joining myself

validation is always available
there's always going to be someone out there
who likes the shade of your shirt or your eyes
confidence is knowing that
and knowing you don't need it to thrive

slowly she let her confidence remove "do you think they"
out of her vocabulary and lived happily ever after

she knew her seasons of sadness would pass
and the sun would soak her skin into gold

growth

sometimes i wish i could go back to the day before i met you
the last day i had with myself
i'd like to meet her one more time
and ask her what it means to be truly happy
because although the new me is stronger and wiser
she paid for the upgrade in pain
i can't help but reminisce about my naive joyful oblivion
but it's okay now i've accepted things will never be the same

failure is only possible if you believe you have
otherwise it is a lie that wants to be believed

pain is the preacher of desire
instead of letting it consume you
ask yourself what it is asking for
what is it trying to teach me?

when you start putting your power in the hands of others
realize they can run away at any moment
don't give handouts
your power lives in your mindset
don't let it leave home

no obstacles can outnumber you
if you count your blessings instead

to believe in yourself
is to become deaf to opinion
blind to judgment
to feel warm even under the thumb of the cold-hearted
to savour your wishes
and to recognize the smell of success regardless of whiffs of
disappointment

how can i see myself as beautiful?

it is not only on the days when i am at my best
when i have gotten nine hours of beauty rest
when my spirits are high
and my makeup is painted like the morning sky
when i have received compliments on my dress
that make me feel as though i am not less
no, it is not only then
it is when the moon seems to overpower the sun
when the days are dark and i can barely manage to put my hair in a
bun
when texts go unanswered
and i am running low on face creams and beauty enhancers
when being productive feels like a dream
and reality hits harder than it used to seem
when my stomach is bloated
and my nails aren't coated
i will see myself more beautiful on these days
because no matter what day it is on the calendar
my beauty is worthy of praise

stop worrying about what they think
remember when they close their eyes at night and blink

they dream of their problems, not yours
people will come in and out of your life like revolving doors
but you hold the power of your worth
you have the ability to hold it up and say

"this is not yours"

i am not of ashamed of being too much

to handle
to carry
to hold

because i know the value of my weight
and there is no room for scales of inadequacy

do not fear living outside the lines
a happy life is not meant to be traced
but painted with a flexible brush

to be confident is not just to look in the mirror and say i am pretty
it is to walk into the room and be excited to speak of your witty
it is to make the first move
whether talking to that girl or guy or showing who's boss when you
got something to prove
it is being inspired by rejection
and not letting it taint your reflection
it is being able to move on with or without closure
and keeping it classy and maintaining your composure
it is to look at fear
and laugh at its intentions because your mind is able to break through
any self-made tension
it is taking any situation
and growing gardens with seeds
it's looking at any problem
and saying "i got this, i am the one i truly need"

never neglect your goals
because you are waiting for love to make you feel full

have faith in knowing love wants to chase you
but you have to start running for your purpose first

dedication is more powerful than motivation
motivation says "today i feel like it"
dedication speaks for today and tomorrow and says "regardless i will
get it done"

i want to understand who i am right now
not sit back in a chair in my old age and wonder "how"
how didn't i see?
my beauty? my grace? my achievements? "was that really me?"
so today i count my small wins
instead of dwelling and seeing slow progress as sins
i will look in the mirror in awe
look at the beauty in everything i am, in all the wonder i saw
i will walk the streets with my head held high
not punishing myself for going home to feel or having a good cry
i am human and unapologetically me
i will not apologize for what sets my spirit free

do not fear walking away
because although it might feel as though you're leaving home
you are actually on a journey to find it

changing your mind is not a sin
but a sign
you are allowed to outgrow
what doesn't let you grow

accomplishments will never heal a broken heart
only love that is homemade

what you choose to see
is what your eyes will endure

slow down
no matter how many cars you see speeding
the finish line is a myth
you'll always want more
if you don't learn to appreciate the stop signs

it is not weak to be vulnerable
it is weak to think that bottling your tears will help you sail
courageously
one day you will have to open the lid

don't risk drowning because you fear a few storms

i encourage you to kill your ego
rather than keeping the what ifs alive
to die with regret is a life not lived

i hope you realize the love i gave you
i will never take back
use it to grow
use it when you forget how amazing you are
use it to spread to others
just because we no longer give it to each other
doesn't mean it should go to waste

Made in United States
North Haven, CT
30 November 2022

27548562R00121